FIRST 50 GOSPEL SONGS

YOU SHOULD PLAY ON GUITAR

ISBN 978-1-7051-2492-5

Hal•Leonard®

Visit Hal Leonard Online at
www.halleonard.com

World headquarters, contact:
Hal Leonard
7777 West Bluemound Road
Milwaukee, WI 53213
Email: info@halleonard.com

In Europe, contact:
Hal Leonard Europe Limited
1 Red Place
London, W1K 6PL
Email: info@halleonardeurope.com

In Australia, contact:
Hal Leonard Australia Pty. Ltd.
4 Lentara Court
Cheltenham, Victoria, 3192 Australia
Email: info@halleonard.com.au

Because He Lives

Words and Music by William J. Gaither and Gloria Gaither

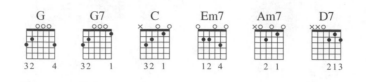

Verse

Moderately

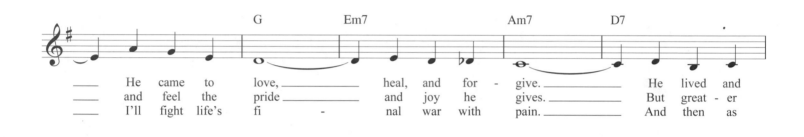

1. God sent His Son, they called Him Je - sus;
hold our new - born ba - by,
day I'll cross the riv - er,

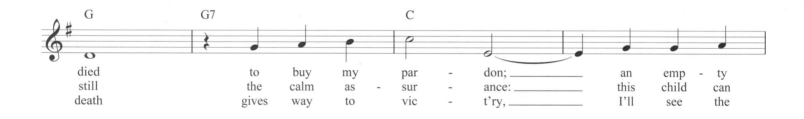

He came to love, heal, and for - give. He lived and
and feel the pride and joy he gives. But great - er
I'll fight life's fi - nal war with pain. And then as

died to buy my par - don; an emp - ty
still the calm as - sur - ance: this child can
death gives way to vic - t'ry, I'll see the

grave is there to prove my Sav - ior lives. Be - cause He
face un - cer - tain days be - cause He lives.
lights of glo - ry and I'll know He reigns.

Chorus

lives I can face to - mor - row, be - cause He lives

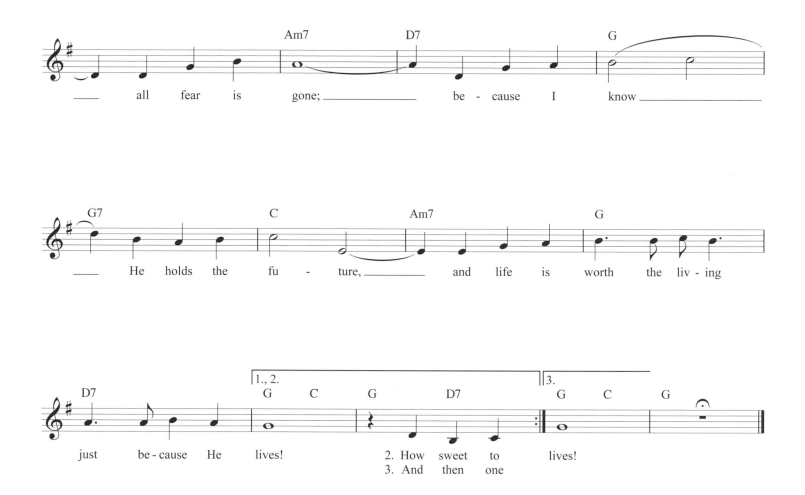

all fear is gone; _____ be - cause I know _____

_____ He holds the fu - ture, _____ and life is worth the liv - ing

just be - cause He lives!

2. How sweet to   lives!
3. And then one

Bind Us Together

Words and Music by Bob Gillman

Bless His Holy Name

Words and Music by Andraé Crouch

The Blood Will Never Lose Its Power

Words and Music by Andraé Crouch

Broken and Spilled Out

Words by Gloria Gaither
Music by Bill George

Verse
Moderately

1. One day ___ a plain vil-lage wom-an. driv-en ___ by love for her Lord, ___ reck-less-ly poured out ___ a val-u-'ble es-sence, dis-re-gard-ing ___ the scorn. ___ And once it was bro-ken ___ and spilled out, a fra-grance filled all ___ the room; ___ ___ like a pris-'ner ___ re-leased from ___ his shack-les, ___ like a

Church in the Wildwood

Words and Music by Dr. William S. Pitts

Down at the Cross
(Glory to His Name)

Words by Elisha A. Hoffman
Music by John H. Stockton

Verse
Moderately fast

1. Down at the cross where the Sav - ior died, down where for
2. I am so won - drous - ly saved from sin, Je - sus so
3. Oh, pre - cious foun - tain that saves from sin, I am so
4. Come to the foun - tain so rich and sweet, cast thy poor

cleans - ing from sin I cried, there to my heart was the
sweet - ly a - bides with - in, there at the cross where He
glad I have en - tered in; there Je - sus saves me and
soul at the Sav - ior's feet; plunge in to - day and be

blood ap - plied,
took me in;
keeps me clean;
made com - plete;

glo - ry to His name! _____

Chorus

Glo - ry to His name, _____ glo - ry to His

name! _____ There to my heart was the blood ap - plied;

1., 2., 3.
glo - ry to his name! _____

4.
name! _____

Give Me That Old Time Religion

Traditional

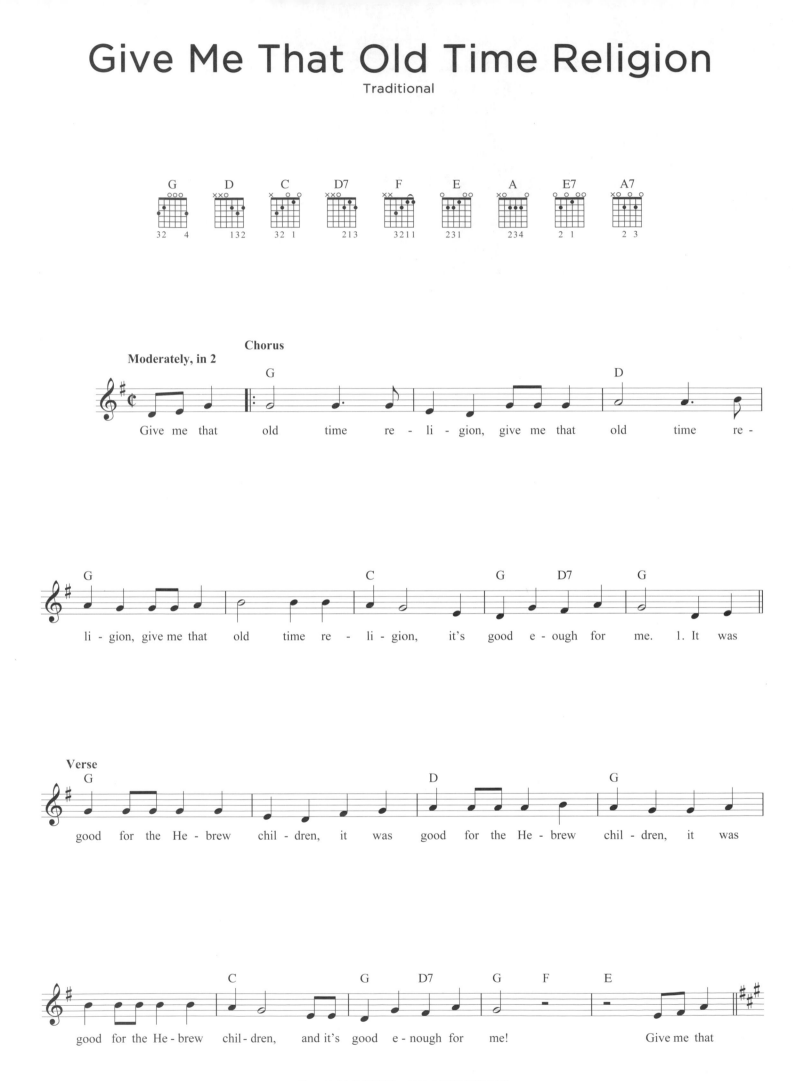

He Looked Beyond My Fault and Saw My Need

Words and Music by Dottie Rambo

He Touched Me

Words and Music by William J. Gaither

He's Got the Whole World in His Hands

Traditional Spiritual

His Name Is Wonderful

Words and Music by Audrey Mieir

His Eye Is on the Sparrow

Words by Civilla D. Martin
Music by Charles H. Gabriel

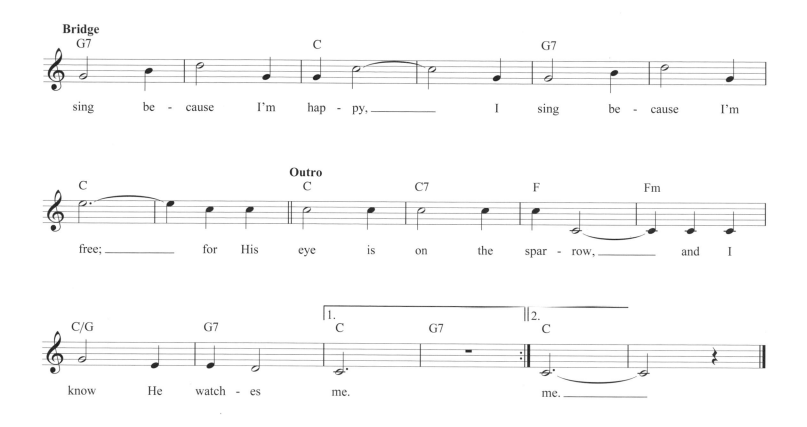

Bridge

G7   C   G7

sing   be - cause   I'm   hap - py, _____   I   sing   be - cause   I'm

Outro

C   C   C7   F   Fm

free; _____   for   His   eye   is   on   the   spar - row, _____   and   I

C/G   G7   1. C   G7   2. C

know   He   watch - es   me.   me. _____

Holy Ground

Words and Music by Geron Davis

How Great Thou Art

Words by Stuart K. Hine
Swedish Folk Melody Adapted and Arranged by Stuart K. Hine

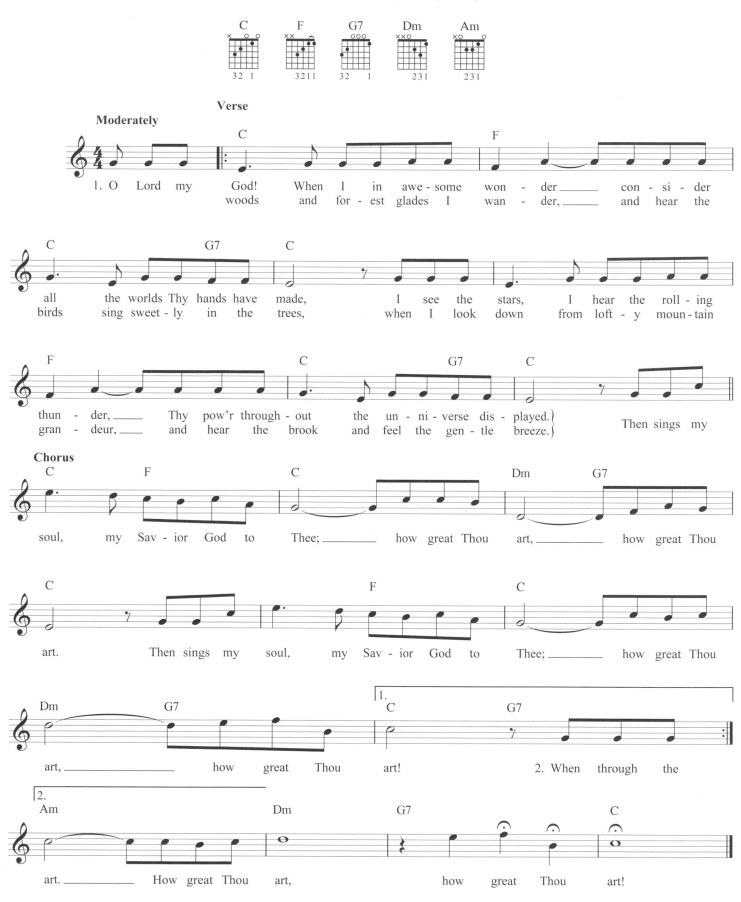

I Believe

Words and Music by Ervin Drake, Jimmy Shirl, Irvin Graham and Al Stillman

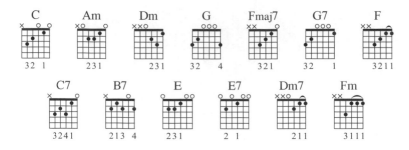

I Bowed on My Knees and Cried Holy

Words by Nettie Washington
Music by E.M. Dudley Cantwell

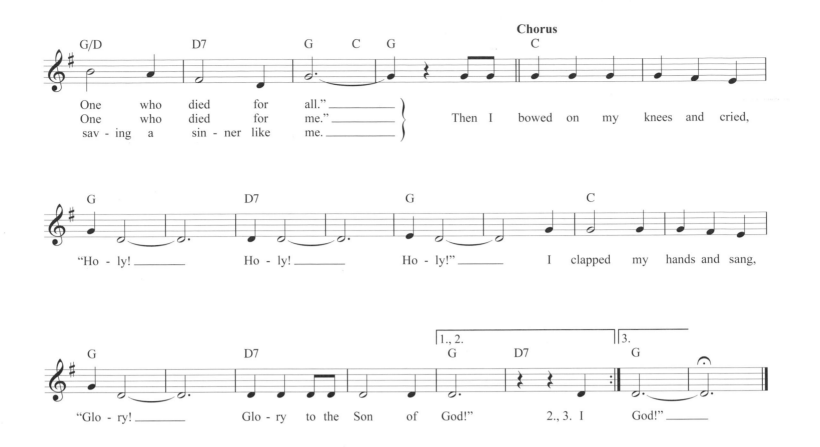

I Saw the Light

Words and Music by Hank Williams

I Will Serve Thee

Words by William J. and Gloria Gaither
Music by William J. Gaither

I'd Rather Have Jesus

Words by Rhea F. Miller
Music by George Beverly Shea

Verse
Modereately

1. I'd rath - er have Je - sus___ than sil - ver or gold, I'd rath - er be
rath - er have Je - sus___ than men's ap - plause, I'd rath - er be
fair - er than lil - ies___ of rar - est bloom, He's sweet - er than

His than have rich - es un - told; I'd rath - er have Je - sus than
faith - ful to His___ dear cause; I'd rath - er have Je - sus than
hon - ey from out___ the comb; He's all that my hun - ger - ing

hous - es or land, I'd rath - er be led by His nail - pierced hand
world - wide fame, I'd rath - er be true to His ho - ly name } than to
spir - it needs, I'd rath - er have Je - sus and let Him lead

Chorus

be the king of a vast do - main or be held in sin's dread

sway!___ I'd rath - er have Je - sus___ than an - y - thing this___

world af - fords to - day.___ 2. I'd day.___
3. He's

I'll Fly Away

Words and Music by Albert E. Brumley

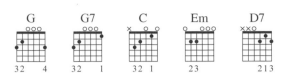

In the Garden

Words and Music by C. Austin Miles

Just a Closer Walk with Thee

Traditional

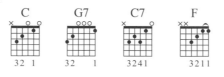

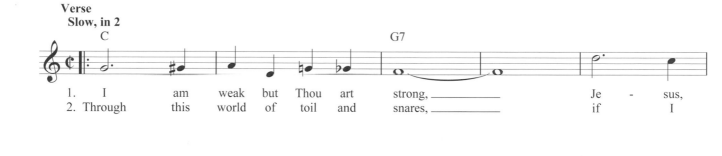

Verse
Slow, in 2

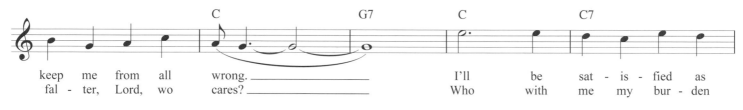

1. I am weak but Thou art strong, _____ Je - sus,
2. Through this world of toil and snares, _____ if I

keep me from all wrong. _____ I'll be sat - is - fied as
fal - ter, Lord, wo cares? _____ Who with me my bur - den

long _____ as I walk let me walk close to Thee. _____
shares? _____ None but Thee, dear Lord, none but Thee. _____

Chorus

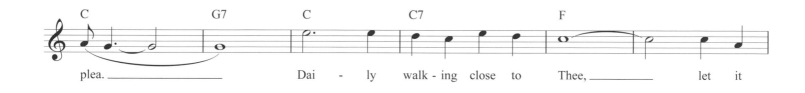

Just a clos - er walk with Thee, _____ grant it Je - sus, is my

plea. _____ Dai - ly walk - ing close to Thee, _____ let it

be, dear Lord, let it be. _____ be. _____

The King Is Coming

Words by William J. and Gloria Gaither and Charles Millhuff
Music by William J. Gaither

Learning to Lean

Words and Music by John Stallings

The Longer I Serve Him

Words and Music by William J. Gaither

Mansion Over the Hilltop

Words and Music by Ira F. Stanphill

Midnight Cry

Words and Music by Greg Day and Chuck Day

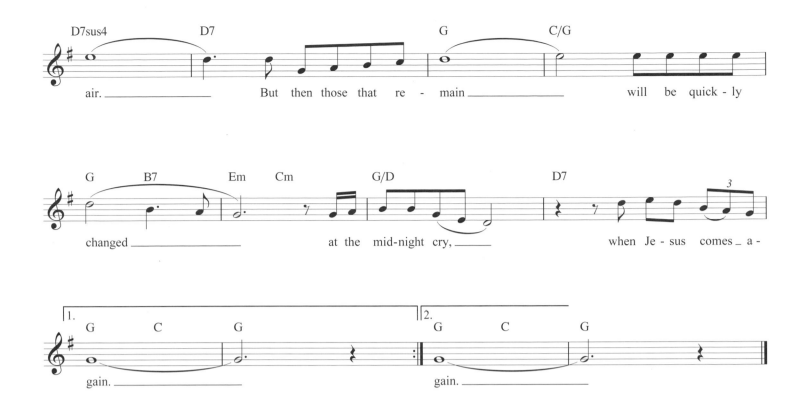

air. _____ But then those that re - main _____ will be quick - ly

changed _____ at the mid-night cry, _____ when Je - sus comes _ a -

1. gain. _____ 2. gain. _____

My Tribute

Words and Music by Andraé Crouch

life; _____ let it be pleas-ing, Lord, to Thee. And should I gain an-y praise, let it go to

Outro

Cal - va - ry. With His blood He has saved me, with His pow'r He has

raised me. To God be the glo - ry for the things He has done!

The Old Rugged Cross

Words and Music by Rev. George Bennard

Precious Lord, Take My Hand
(Take My Hand, Precious Lord)

Words and Music by Thomas A. Dorsey

Precious Memories

Words and Music by J.B.F. Wright

Reach Out to Jesus

Words and Music by Ralph Carmichael

Put Your Hand in the Hand

Words and Music by Gene MacLellan

Room at the Cross for You

Words and Music by Ira F. Stanphill

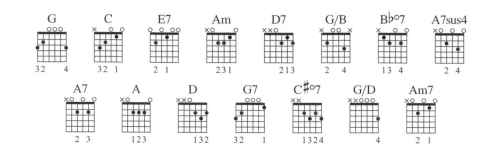

Verse
Moderately slow

1. The cross up-on which Je - sus died _____ is a shel - ter in
mil - lions have found Him a friend _____ and have turned from the

which we can hide. _____ And its grace so free is suf - fi - cient for
sins they have sinned, _____ the _ Sav - ior still waits to _ o - pen the

me, and deep is its foun - tan, _____ as wide as _____ the sea. } There's
gate, and wel - come a sin - ner _____ be - fore it's _____ too late. }

Chorus

room at the cross for you, _____ there's room at the cross for you. _____

_____ Though mil - lions have come, there's still room for one, yes, there's

[1. room at the cross for you. _____ [2.]

2. Though you. _____

Shall We Gather at the River?

Words and Music by Robert Lowry

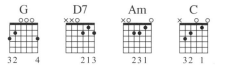

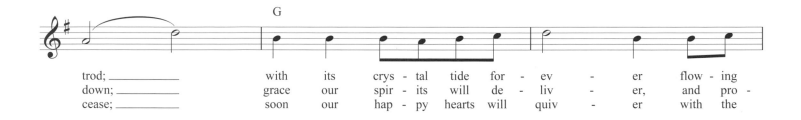

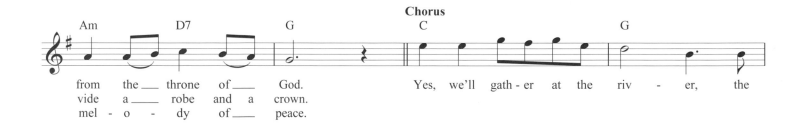

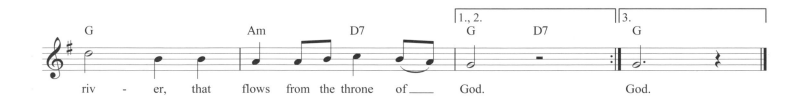

Sheltered in the Arms of God

Words and Music by Dottie Rambo and Jimmie Davis

Soon and Very Soon

Words and Music by Andraé Crouch

Sweet By and By

Words by Sanford Fillmore Bennett
Music by Joseph P. Webster

Sweet, Sweet Spirit

Words and Music by Doris Akers

Swing Low, Sweet Chariot

Traditional Spiritual

There Will Be Peace in the Valley for Me

Words and Music by Thomas A. Dorsey

Verse

Moderately

G

1. I am ti - red and wea - ry but I must toil on till the
flow'rs will be bloom - in', the grass will be green, and the
bear will be gen - tle, the wolf will be tame, and the

Lord comes to call me a - way, where the morn - ing is bright and the
skies will be clear and se - rene. The sun ev - er shines, giv - ing
lion will lay down with the lamb. The host from the wild will be

Lamb is the light and the night is as fair as the day.
one end - less beam and no clouds there will ev - er be seen.
led by a Child, I'll be changed from the crea - ture I am. There'll be

Chorus

peace in the val - ley for me some - day, there'll be peace in the val - ley for

me, I pray. No sor - row and sad - ness or trou - ble will be, there'll be

1., 2.
peace in the val - ley for me. 2., 3. There the

3.
me.

There's Something About That Name

Words by William J. and Gloria Gaither
Music by William J. Gaither

Victory in Jesus

Words and Music by E.M. Bartlett

Turn Your Radio On

Words and Music by Albert E. Brumley

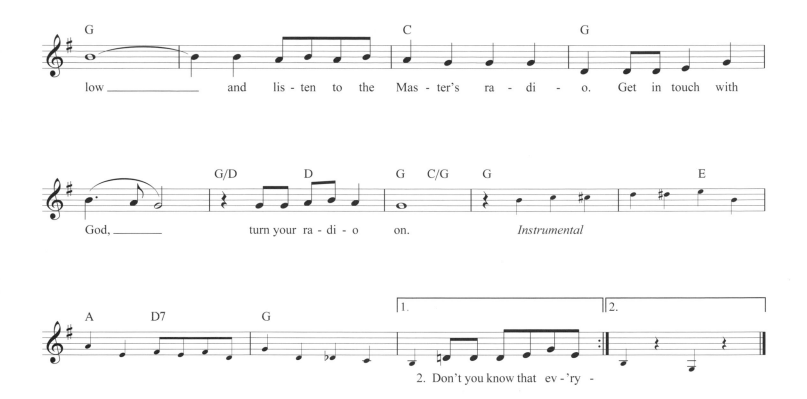

low _____ and lis-ten to the Mas-ter's ra-di-o. Get in touch with

God, _____ turn your ra-di-o on. *Instrumental*

2. Don't you know that ev-'ry-

Wayfaring Stranger

Southern American Folk Hymn

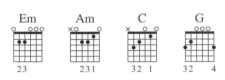

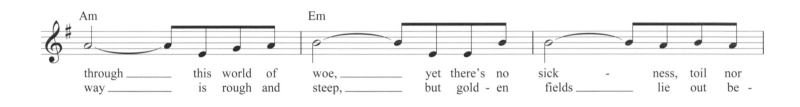

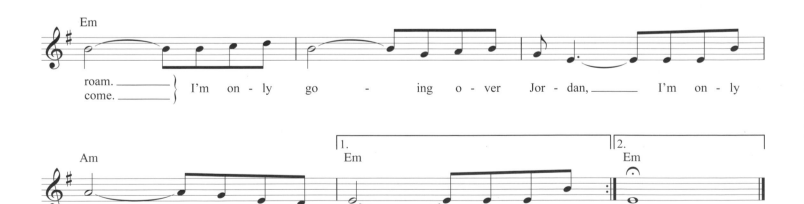

When the Saints Go Marching In

Words by Katherine E. Purvis
Music by James M. Black

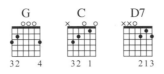

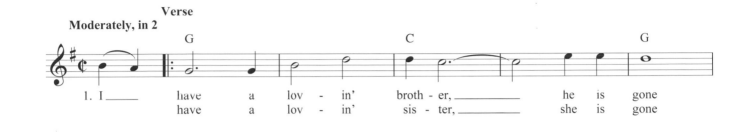

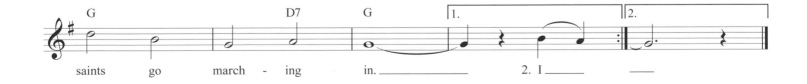

Whispering Hope

Words and Music by Alice Hawthorne

Wings of a Dove

Words and Music by Bob Ferguson

Wonderful Grace of Jesus

Words and Music by Haldor Lillenas

FIRST 50

Books in the First 50 series contain easy to intermediate arrangements for must-know songs. Each arrangement is simple and streamlined, yet still captures the essence of the tune.

First 50 Baroque Pieces
You Should Play on Guitar

Includes selections by Johann Sebastian Bach, Robert de Visée, Ernst Gottlieb Baron, Santiago de Murcia, Antonio Vivaldi, Sylvius Leopold Weiss, and more.
00322567..$14.99

First 50 Bluegrass Solos
You Should Play on Guitar

I Am a Man of Constant Sorrow • Long Journey Home • Molly and Tenbrooks • Old Joe Clark • Rocky Top • Salty Dog Blues • and more.
00298574..$16.99

First 50 Blues Songs
You Should Play on Guitar

All Your Love (I Miss Loving) • Bad to the Bone • Born Under a Bad Sign • Dust My Broom • Hoodoo Man Blues • Little Red Rooster • Love Struck Baby • Pride and Joy • Smoking Gun • Still Got the Blues • The Thrill Is Gone • You Shook Me • and more.
00235790..$17.99

First 50 Blues Turnarounds
You Should Play on Guitar

You'll learn cool turnarounds in the styles of these jazz legends: John Lee Hooker, Robert Johnson, Joe Pass, Jimmy Rogers, Hubert Sumlin, Stevie Ray Vaughan, T-Bone Walker, Muddy Waters, and more.
00277469..$14.99

First 50 Chords
You Should Play on Guitar

American Pie • Back in Black • Brown Eyed Girl • Landslide • Let It Be • Riptide • Summer of '69 • Take Me Home, Country Roads • Won't Get Fooled Again • You've Got a Friend • and more.
00300255 Guitar..$12.99

First 50 Classical Pieces
You Should Play on Guitar

Includes compositions by J.S. Bach, Augustin Barrios, Matteo Carcassi, Domenico Scarlatti, Fernando Sor, Francisco Tárrega, Robert de Visée, Antonio Vivaldi and many more.
00155414..$16.99

First 50 Folk Songs
You Should Play on Guitar

Amazing Grace • Down by the Riverside • Home on the Range • I've Been Working on the Railroad • Kumbaya • Man of Constant Sorrow • Oh! Susanna • This Little Light of Mine • When the Saints Go Marching In • The Yellow Rose of Texas • and more.
00235868..$16.99

First 50 Guitar Duets
You Should Play

Chopsticks • Clocks • Eleanor Rigby • Game of Thrones Theme • Hallelujah • Linus and Lucy (from *A Charlie Brown Christmas*) • Memory (from *Cats*) • Over the Rainbow (from *The Wizard of Oz*) • Star Wars (Main Theme) • What a Wonderful World • You Raise Me Up • and more.
00319706..$14.99

First 50 Jazz Standards
You Should Play on Guitar

All the Things You Are • Body and Soul • Don't Get Around Much Anymore • Fly Me to the Moon (In Other Words) • The Girl from Ipanema (Garota De Ipanema) • I Got Rhythm • Laura • Misty • Night and Day • Satin Summertime • When I Fall in Love • and more.
00198594 Solo Guitar..$16.99

First 50 Kids' Songs
You Should Play on Guitar

Do-Re-Mi • Hakuna Matata • Let It Go • My Favorite Things • Puff the Magic Dragon • Take Me Out to the Ball Game • Won't You Be My Neighbor? (It's a Beautiful Day in the Neighborhood) • and more.
00300500..$15.99

First 50 Licks
You Should Play on Guitar

Licks presented include the styles of legendary guitarists like Eric Clapton, Buddy Guy, Jimi Hendrix, B.B. King, Randy Rhoads, Carlos Santana, Stevie Ray Vaughan and many more.
00278875 Book/Online Audio..$14.99

First 50 Riffs
You Should Play on Guitar

All Right Now • Back in Black • Barracuda • Carry on Wayward Son • Crazy Train • La Grange • Layla • Seven Nation Army • Smoke on the Water • Sunday Bloody Sunday • Sunshine of Your Love • Sweet Home Alabama • Working Man • and more.
00277366..$14.99

First 50 Rock Songs You Should
Play on Electric Guitar

All Along the Watchtower • Beat It • Brown Eyed Girl • Cocaine • Detroit Rock City • Hallelujah • (I Can't Get No) Satisfaction • Oh, Pretty Woman • Pride and Joy • Seven Nation Army • Should I Stay or Should I Go • Smells like Teen Spirit • Smoke on the Water • When I Come Around • You Really Got Me • and more.
00131159..$15.99

First 50 Songs by the Beatles You
Should Play on Guitar

All You Need Is Love • Blackbird • Come Together • Eleanor Rigby • Hey Jude • I Want to Hold Your Hand • Let It Be • Ob-La-Di, Ob-La-Da • She Loves You • Twist and Shout • Yellow Submarine • Yesterday • and more.
00295323..$19.99

First 50 Songs
You Should Fingerpick on Guitar

Annie's Song • Blackbird • The Boxer • Classical Gas • Dust in the Wind • Fire and Rain • Greensleeves • Road Trippin' • Shape of My Heart • Tears in Heaven • Time in a Bottle • Vincent (Starry Starry Night) • and more.
00149269..$16.99

First 50 Songs You Should
Play on 12-String Guitar

California Dreamin' • Closer to the Heart • Free Fallin' • Give a Little Bit • Hotel California • Leaving on a Jet Plane • Life by the Drop • Over the Hills and Far Away • Solsbury Hill • Space Oddity • Wish You Were Here • You Wear It Well • and more.
00287559..$15.99

First 50 Songs You Should Play on
Acoustic Guitar

Against the Wind • Boulevard of Broken Dreams • Champagne Supernova • Every Rose Has Its Thorn • Fast Car • Free Fallin' • Layla • Let Her Go • Mean • One • Ring of Fire • Signs • Stairway to Heaven • Trouble • Wagon Wheel • Yellow • Yesterday • and more.
00131209..$16.99

First 50 Songs
You Should Play on Bass

Blister in the Sun • I Got You (I Feel Good) • Livin' on a Prayer • Low Rider • Money • Monkey Wrench • My Generation • Roxanne • Should I Stay or Should I Go • Uptown Funk • What's Going On • With or Without You • Yellow • and more.
00149189..$16.99

First 50 Songs
You Should Play on Solo Guitar

Africa • All of Me • Blue Skies • California Dreamin' • Change the World • Crazy • Dream a Little Dream of Me • Every Breath You Take • Hallelujah • Wonderful Tonight • Yesterday • You Raise Me Up • Your Song • and more.
00288843..$17.99

First 50 Songs
You Should Strum on Guitar

American Pie • Blowin' in the Wind • Daughter • Hey, Soul Sister • Home • I Will Wait • Losing My Religion • Mrs. Robinson • No Woman No Cry • Peaceful Easy Feeling • Rocky Mountain High • Sweet Caroline • Teardrops on My Guitar • Wonderful Tonight • and more.
00148996 Guitar..$16.99

HAL•LEONARD®
www.halleonard.com

1022
014

Prices, contents and availability subject to change without notice.

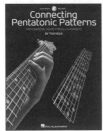

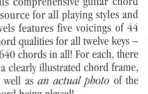